Hey Badass!! Welcome to your new workbook!

I'm so happy that you are taking action and preparing for major success in your career! You are truly an inspiration to me and to those around you!!

I have designed this workbook to help you set BIG Goals and get ready for your job search and interviews.

It will help you get organized, reflect on your goals, document your thoughts, identify your strengths and areas of opportunity, capture your amazing accomplishments and incredible experience examples, identify mentors, help you update your resume, kick off your job search, get you into the right mindset, and prepare you to ROCK your upcoming job interviews.

You'll find plenty of writing space throughout your workbook so you can keep coming back to it to document your thoughts.

Not quite ready to start your job search? No worries, you can easily start capturing your story now so you'll be prepared when it's time.

I wish you all the best in your career journey and I know YOU ARE GOING TO DO GREAT THINGS!!

Tabatha

Limits Exist
Only In The
Mind.

badass

noun [bad- ass]

A person in control, taking charge of their own circumstances in work and life. One who knows their worth and won't accept anything less.

What are your career goals, dreams, and ambitions? Think long term and short term. For each goal, add notes about what you need to do to achieve the goal. Do you need more education, experience, time, mentorship, etc.

What small things can you do now to start taking steps forward?

"If you don't know where you're going, how will you ever get there?"

My 10-year career goals are...

Steps I need to take in order to achieve my 10-year goals:

My 5-year career goals are...

Steps I need to take in order to achieve my 5-year goals:

My 3-year career goals are:

Steps I need to take in order to achieve my 3-year goals:

My 1-year career goals are:

Steps I need to take in order to achieve my 1-year goals:

Break the steps down into quarterly and monthly goals to

make it simple.

Steps I need to take in order to achieve my 1-year goals:
Break the steps down into quarterly and monthly goals to
make it simple.

What can I do today to start taking action toward my goals?

What can I do today to start taking action toward my goals?

What can I do today to start taking action toward my goals?

Often, we don't work on our goals because we feel that something is standing in the way.

Sometimes it's fear-of success or fear of failure.

Either way, fear has a way of making us feel stuck in place. Let's get unstuck-What is standing in your way?

Take some time to review your goals and think about:

1. What's the worst thing that could happen if I don't move forward on this?

2. What's the worst thing that could happen if I go for it and it doesn't work out?

3. What's the BEST THING that could happen if I succeed?

4. How am I going to feel 1 year from now if I don't at least try?

What is standing in the way? What is making me feel stuck

and unable to move forward toward my goals?

What is standing in the way? What is making me feel stuck

and unable to move forward toward my goals?

What is standing in the way? What is making me feel stuck

and unable to move forward toward my goals?

What is standing in the way? What is making me feel stuck

and unable to move forward toward my goals?

What is standing in the way? What is making me feel stuck and unable to move forward toward my goals?

Now let's talk about the future and what moving forward will look and feel like.

Close your eyes and envision yourself, living your life 1 year from now.

Envision yourself working in your new job.

- *What is different about you?*

- *How do you feel?*

- *What can this future version of you do that today's version cannot?*

- *What is the impact to your relationships?*

- *What will you have that you don't have today?*

In 1 year from now, things will be very different if you put in the work. Use the following pages to capture your thoughts and vision of you 1 year from now.

In 1 year from now, things will be very different if you put in the work. Use the following pages to capture your thoughts and vision of you 1 year from now.

In 1 year from now, things will be very different if you put in the work. Use the following pages to capture your thoughts and vision of you 1 year from now.

*In 1 year from now, things will be very different if you put
in the work. Use the following pages to capture your
thoughts and vision of you 1 year from now.*

In 1 year from now, things will be very different if you put in the work. Use the following pages to capture your thoughts and vision of you 1 year from now.

On the next pages, you will be writing down information that will help you prepare for your job search, resume updates, networking, and job interviews.

Take your time and capture the details that are important to you.

You can always go back and add more notes.

Are there companies you dream of working for?

Jot down the names of the companies and some notes about why you want to work there.

Do you know someone who works there now? If so, reach out and ask to schedule an informational interview.

"Network early and network often; you never know what doors networking may open for you."

I dream about working at the following companies:

Who can I reach out to for more information about these companies?

Don't wait until you need something to start building and nurturing your network.

LinkedIn is an excellent networking platform. Connect with 3 new people and reach out to 3 existing connections every month.

"It's not always about who youknow...but sometimes it is."

I will connect with 3 NEW people each month -

Keep track and stay in touch.

I will connect with 3 NEW people each month -

Keep track and stay in touch.

I will connect with 3 NEW people each month -

Keep track and stay in touch.

I will connect with 3 EXISTING people in my network each month-

Contact 3 existing people and schedule a virtual coffee break.

I will connect with 3 EXISTING people in my network each month-

Contact 3 existing people and schedule a virtual coffee break.

I will connect with 3 EXISTING people in my network each month-

Contact 3 existing people and schedule a virtual coffee break.

What are you truly AMAZING
at? What are your special skills?

In what areas do you
consider yourself an expert?

*"It's ok to brag about yourself. If you
don't, who will?"*

I'm AMAZING at these things:

I'm AMAZING at these things:

Think about your career accomplishments.

I am most proud of... add stats and metrics if you can

Think about your career accomplishments.

I am most proud of... add stats and metrics if you can

Next, focus on everything you LOVE to do. This can be a combination of soft skills, technical skills, hobbies, special interests, anything you love to do at work and outside of work.

"Find a way to do what you love at work. It's a lot more fun that way."

What am I passionate about? What ignites the fire inside of me?

What am I passionate about? What ignites the fire inside of me?

You are unique and special in many ways. What do you bring to the workplace that is unique and special?

"Don't ever forget how awesome you are."

The best way I can describe myself is...

If you get stuck or run out of words, ask friends, family and

coworkers for help.

The best way I can describe myself is...

If you get stuck or run out of words, ask friends, family and

coworkers for help.

People love working with me because...

Think about compliments from coworkers, leaders, friends. What

do you bring to the workplace that people love?

People love working with me because...

Think about compliments from coworkers, leaders, friends. What

do you bring to the workplace that people love?

Describe yourself as a Leader.

What do you love the most about leading people?

What are some things you are trying to improve?

What are your areas of weakness? What are you doing to overcome them?

"No one is perfect, each of us is a work in progress."

Hint-Feedback is a valuable gift. Ask your leader, peers and teammates for 1 piece of positive feedback and 1 piece of constructive feedback

Feedback I received:

Feedback I received:

Feedback I received:

I am working to get better at...

Who are my mentors? Who can I trust to give me career advice?

How can my mentors help me improve?

Who are my mentors? Who can I trust to give me career advice?

How can my mentors help me improve?

When you are seeking new employment, you should be prepared to respond to behavioral interview questions.

The best way to do this is to document examples of your experience.

Use the following pages to capture your examples. Think about:

1. *What was the situation?*
2. *What specifically did you do to manage the situation?*
3. *What did you learn from the situation?*
4. *What was the outcome?*

"95% of your confidence during a job interview is a direct result of being prepared."

Example of a time when you had a conflict with a coworker or boss:

1. What was the situation?

2. What specifically did you do to manage the situation?

3. What did you learn from the situation?

4. What was the outcome?

Example of a time when you had a conflict with a coworker or boss:

1. What was the situation?

2. What specifically did you do to manage the situation?

3. What did you learn from the situation?

4. What was the outcome?

Example of a time when you had to communicate a difficult message

1. *What was the situation?*

2. *What specifically did you do to manage the situation?*

3. *What did you learn from the situation?*

4. *What was the outcome?*

Example of a time when you had to communicate a difficult message to your team.

1. *What was the situation?*

2. *What specifically did you do to manage the situation?*

3. *What did you learn from the situation?*

4. *What was the outcome?*

Example of a time when you demonstrated leadership:

1. What was the situation?

2. What specifically did you do to manage the situation?

3. What did you learn from the situation?

4. What was the outcome?

Example of a time when you demonstrated leadership:

1. What was the situation?

2. What specifically did you do to manage the situation?

3. What did you learn from the situation?

4. What was the outcome?

Example of a time when you demonstrated teamwork:

1. What was the situation?

2. What specifically did you do to manage the situation?

3. What did you learn from the situation?

4. What was the outcome?

Example of a time when you demonstrated teamwork:

1. What was the situation?

2. What specifically did you do to manage the situation?

3. What did you learn from the situation?

4. What was the outcome?

Example of a time when you went against the popular opinion at work:

1. What was the situation?

2. What specifically did you do to manage the situation?

3. What did you learn from the situation?

4. What was the outcome?

Example of a time when you went against the popular opinion at

Work.

1. *What was the situation?*

2. *What specifically did you do to manage the situation?*

3. *What did you learn from the situation?*

4. *What was the outcome?*

Example of a time when you missed a deadline:

1. What was the situation?

2. What specifically did you do to manage the situation?

3. What did you learn from the situation?

4. What was the outcome?

Example of a time when you missed a deadline:

1. *What was the situation?*

2. *What specifically did you do to manage the situation?*

3. *What did you learn from the situation?*

4. *What was the outcome?*

Example of a time when you failed at something:

1. What was the situation?

2. What specifically did you do to manage the situation?

3. What did you learn from the situation?

4. What was the outcome?

Example of a time when you failed at something:

1. What was the situation?

2. What specifically did you do to manage the situation?

3. What did you learn from the situation?

4. What was the outcome?

Example of a time when you coached someone:

   1. What was the situation?

   2. What specifically did you do to manage the situation?

   3. What did you learn from the situation?

   4. What was the outcome?

Example of a time when you coached someone:

1. What was the situation?

2. What specifically did you do to manage the situation?

3. What did you learn from the situation?

4. What was the outcome?

Example of a time when you had to go above and beyond to complete

a project on time:

1. *What was the situation?*

2. *What specifically did you do to manage the situation?*

3. *What did you learn from the situation?*

4. *What was the outcome?*

Example of a time when you had to go above and beyond to complete

a project on time:

1. What was the situation?

2. What specifically did you do to manage the situation?

3. What did you learn from the situation?

4. What was the outcome?

Example of a time when you provided a coworker with feedback:

1. What was the situation?

2. What specifically did you do to manage the situation?

3. What did you learn from the situation?

4. What was the outcome?

Example of a time when you provided a coworker with feedback:

1. What was the situation?

2. What specifically did you do to manage the situation?

3. What did you learn from the situation?

4. What was the outcome?

Example of a time when you disagreed with your boss:

1. What was the situation?

2. What specifically did you do to manage the situation?

3. What did you learn from the situation?

4. What was the outcome?

Example of a time when you disagreed with your boss:

1. What was the situation?

2. What specifically did you do to manage the situation?

3. What did you learn from the situation?

4. What was the outcome?

Example of a time when you were asked to do something outside of your normal job duties:

1. *What was the situation?*

2. *What specifically did you do to manage the situation?*

3. *What did you learn from the situation?*

4. *What was the outcome?*

Example of a time when you were asked to do something outside of your normal job duties:

1. What was the situation?

2. What specifically did you do to manage the situation?

3. What did you learn from the situation?

4. What was the outcome?

Example of a time when you missed a deadline:

  1. *What was the situation?*

  2. *What specifically did you do to manage the situation?*

  3. *What did you learn from the situation?*

  4. *What was the outcome?*

Example of a time when you missed a deadline:

1. What was the situation?

2. What specifically did you do to manage the situation?

3. What did you learn from the situation?

4. What was the outcome?

Example of a time when took the lead on a project:

1. What was the situation?

2. What specifically did you do to manage the situation?

3. What did you learn from the situation?

4. What was the outcome?

Example of a time when took the lead on a project:

1. What was the situation?

2. What specifically did you do to manage the situation?

3. What did you learn from the situation?

4. What was the outcome?

What is important to you when it comes to Workplace Culture:

Employee Experience, Positive Brand, Diversity, Development, Advancement Opportunities, Recognition, other

"The culture of a company is one of the biggest drivers of employee loyalty"

Workplace culture aspects that are important to me:

What are hard stops for me? Things I dislike and do not want in my

next position.

Sometimes the job search can be tough. When days are hard, remember that you are a badass! Find a few quotes that inspire you.

Create a list of the things you are most proud. This is a great way to keep your confidence high!

"You have done so many incredible things. Hard times are just a sign that better things are coming."

Create a list of the 50 thing you are most proud of in your life

and or career:

Keep adding to the list...you know there are more than 50...

Add a new accomplishment every month from today forward.

Positive affirmations are a great way to remind yourself that you are an AMAZING BADASS and that you have so much to be grateful for. Write down a few affirmations that you can read to remind yourself why you are so incredible.

Here's one of mine as an example:

"I am happy and grateful to have a special gift that allows me to help women see themselves as others see them: They are confident, amazing badasses. I feel the most amazing and badass when I'm helping women in this way."

Positive Affirmations to remind myself that I am a BADASS:

Positive Affirmations to remind myself that I am a BADASS:

Positive Affirmations to remind myself that I am a BADASS:

Positive Affirmations to remind myself that I am a BADASS:

When you're feeling stuck, review your goals and remember why you started.

Don't compare your journey to anyone else's journey. You are on the right track...YOUR track!

Journaling is also a great way to get out of your own head. Use the following prompts.

Things I can do to adjust my mindset when I feel stuck are...

I'm grateful for...

When I achieve my goals, I feel...

Things I can do this week that will get me closer to my 10 year goals are...

When I start to compare myself to others, things I can focus on to change my thoughts are...

I love myself because...

What will make today a great day?

When was the last time I enjoyed some self-care? If not in the past 2 weeks, what is 1 thing I can do for myself within the next 24 hours?

What are 10 things that energize or inspire me?

What songs amp up my energy? Are they all on my playlist?

What is the most rewarding thing I have ever done? Why was it

so rewarding?

What is the scariest bravest thing I have ever done?

What did I learn how did I grow from the experience?

What do I wish someone had told me when I was younger?

What things make me happy?

Write about something that is on my mind today.

Take a walk or just sit outside. Write about how I felt before, during, and after.

Write about my hopes and dreams.

Envision myself working in my dream career. How do I feel?

What has improved as a result? How do I feel every day when

I go to work?

Write about my fears and worries. What will happen if I don't push past them? What small steps can I take to move forward so they don't hold me back?

Write about sounds or smells that make me happy.

Write about recent feedback I received at work and how I plan to implement changes or grow.

If I had 24 hours to do whatever I wanted tomorrow, what would I do? What's stopping me from doing it?

If I could spend a day with anyone, living or dead, who would it be and why? What would I want to talk about?

If I could change 1 thing in my life, what would it be?

What's stopping me from changing it now?

What was the best part of my day today? What can I do now to make tomorrow a great day?

How do I know that I am a BADASS? What BADASS

qualities do I demonstrate every day?

Who inspired me today? What did they do?

Who did I inspire today? How did I do it?

Is there someone I need to thank? Who is it and why do I need to thank them?

What can I do this weekend to help me get excited about going to work on Monday?

What are my biggest dreams and who can I share them with?

This week I am going to be exceptional at...

Keep journaling using prompts of your own. Use journaling daily

as a method to remove negativity and stay focused on the positive.

Keep journaling using prompts of your own. Use journaling daily

as a method to remove negativity and stay focused on the positive.

Keep journaling using prompts of your own. Use journaling daily as a method to remove negativity and stay focused on the positive.

Keep journaling using prompts of your own. Use journaling daily as a method to remove negativity and stay focused on the positive.

Keep journaling using prompts of your own. Use journaling daily as a method to remove negativity and stay focused on the positive.

Keep journaling using prompts of your own. Use journaling daily

as a method to remove negativity and stay focused on the positive.

Keep journaling using prompts of your own. Use journaling daily as a method to remove negativity and stay focused on the positive.

Notes to Self: Use the blank pages to track interview notes, feedback, additional career dreams, aspirations, accomplishments, and inspiration.

"Darling, You are an amazing Badass and you have the power to do anything you put your mind to.

Remember to take small steps every day, enjoy your journey, and be kind to yourself."

Notes to Self:

Notes to Self:

Notes to Self:

Notes to Self:

Notes to Self:

Notes to Self:

Notes to Self:

Notes to Self:

Notes to Self:

Notes to Self:

Notes to Self:

Notes to Self:

Notes to Self:

Notes to Self:

Notes to Self:

Notes to Self:

Notes to Self:

Notes to Self:

Notes to Self:

Notes to Self:

I hope you found this journal to be helpful as you prepare to move forward on your career journey and crush your goals!.

By taking the time to set goals, adjust your mindset, and document your experience and accomplishments, you will be well positioned to interview when the time comes.

The next step is to use your notes to update your resume and practice interviewing with a friend.
The more you practice, the more confident you will feel talking about yourself.

Wishing you so much success as you move forward on your journey.

XOXO-Tabatha

More career related advice can be found on my website: www.tabathajones.com.

Made in the USA
Middletown, DE
28 October 2022

13693534R00093